M000086056

A LOVE JOUR

100 Things

I about

GRANDMA

Lisa Carpenter

R
ROCKRIDGE
PRESS

Copyright © 2021 by Rockridge Press, Emeryville, California

No part of this publication may be reproduced, stored in a retrieval system, or transmitted in any form or by any means, electronic, mechanical, photocopying, recording, scanning, or otherwise, except as permitted under Sections 107 or 108 of the 1976 United States Copyright Act, without the prior written permission of the Publisher. Requests to the Publisher for permission should be addressed to the Permissions Department, Rockridge Press, 6005 Shellmound Street, Suite 175, Emeryville, CA 94608.

Limit of Liability/Disclaimer of Warranty: The Publisher and the author make no representations or warranties with respect to the accuracy or completeness of the contents of this work and specifically disclaim all warranties, including without limitation warranties of fitness for a particular purpose. No warranty may be created or extended by sales or promotional materials. The advice and strategies contained herein may not be suitable for every situation. This work is sold with the understanding that the Publisher is not engaged in rendering medical, legal, or other professional advice or services. If professional assistance is required, the services of a competent professional person should be sought. Neither the Publisher nor the author shall be liable for damages arising herefrom. The fact that an individual, organization, or website is referred to in this work as a citation and/or potential source of further information does not mean that the author or the Publisher endorses the information the individual, organization, or website may provide or recommendations they/it may make. Further, readers should be aware that websites listed in this work may have changed or disappeared between when this work was written and when it is read.

For general information on our other products and services or to obtain technical support, please contact our Customer Care Department within the United States at (866) 744-2665, or outside the United States at (510) 253-0500.

Rockridge Press publishes its books in a variety of electronic and print formats. Some content that appears in print may not be available in electronic books, and vice versa.

TRADEMARKS: Rockridge Press and the Rockridge Press logo are trademarks or registered trademarks of Callisto Media Inc. and/or its affiliates, in the United States and other countries, and may not be used without written permission. All other trademarks are the property of their respective owners. Rockridge Press is not associated with any product or vendor mentioned in this book.

Series Designer: Liz Cosgrove
Interior and Cover Designer: Stephanie Mautone
Art Producer: Samantha Ulman
Editor: Carolyn Abate
Production Editor: Matthew Burnett
Production Manager: Riley Hoffman

All images used under license © Shutterstock.

Paperback ISBN: 978-1-63807-343-7
R0

From: ....

To: ....

with lots of love

Date: ....

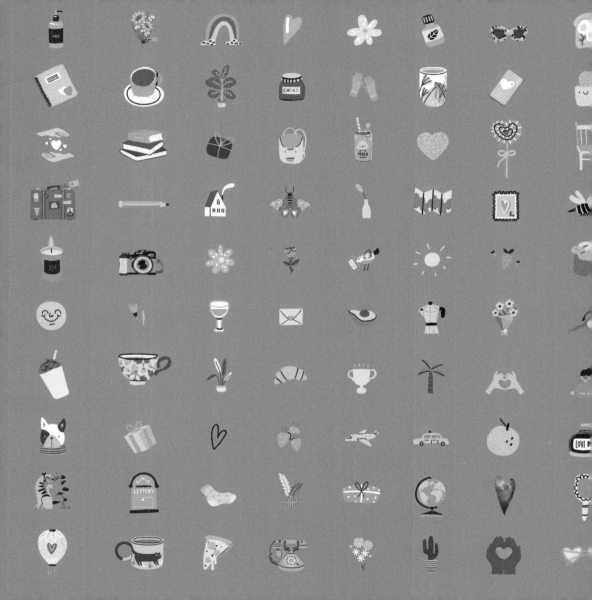

Author's Note

This journal celebrates the special bond between a grandchild and their grandmother—*your* special bond! There have been billions of grandkids and grandmas loving one another throughout history (possibly more!) but there has never been a grandchild–grandma connection quite like yours. Every grandchild, every grandmother, and every bond between the two is unique.

In the following pages, you'll capture the memories, moments, traits, and more you love about your grandma and the one-of-a-kind relationship you share. There are also "extra love" pages throughout that provide room for additional sweet memories, like more details, pictures, or other mementos.

The task ahead requires a few tools. For the grandchild completing the journal, there are two: a pen or pencil to write with and your thinking cap for reaching back in your memory and deep in your heart to fill in the blanks with feeling. For Grandma, there's just one: tissues (lots of them) for managing the leaky-eye side effects that may result when reading this heartfelt keepsake that you'll treasure forever.

Best wishes to you both for a grand time writing and reading!

♡ *Gramma Lisa*

1.

I love when you call me

2.

Your

....

makes me laugh.

3.

WHEN WE SPEND TIME TOGETHER,

I REALLY ENJOY THAT WE

....

4.

You have

....

and

....

in your heart.

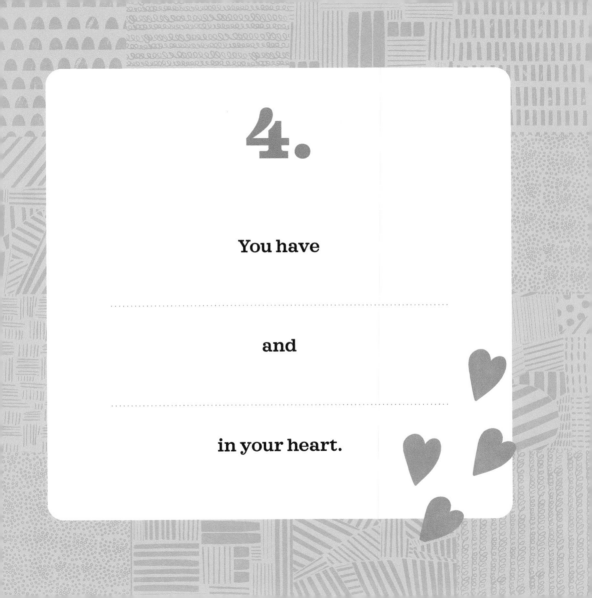

5.

I'm lucky you

....

on my birthdays.

6.

Besides being a grandma, you are a

....

and

....,

too.

7.

My love for you could fill a

....

8.

**The top three things that are better
when I do them with you are . . .**

1.

2.

3.

9.

You deserve an award for

....

"extra love"

10.

EVERY TIME I SEE YOU,

THE FIRST THING I DO IS

....

11.

I love hearing your story about

....

again and again.

12.

I think you

....

when you wear

....

13.

You encourage me to be better at

....

14.

WHEN I WAS LITTLE, YOU WOULD

....

ME.

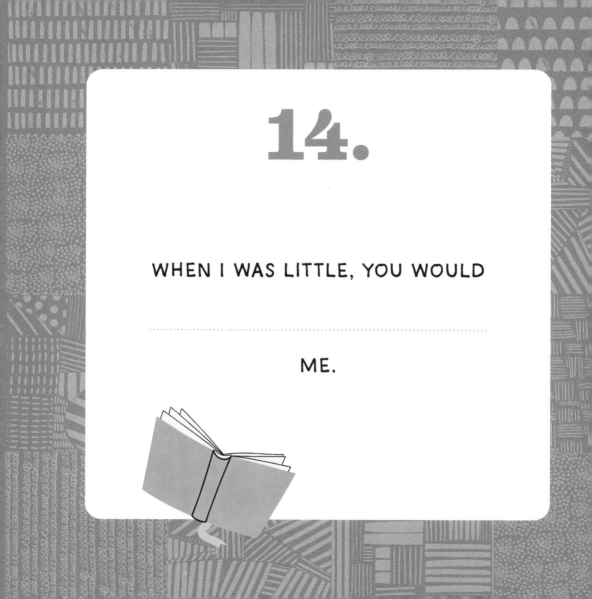

15.

You taught me to

....

when

....

16.

Of all the colors in the rainbow,

....

best matches your personality because

....

17.

Your hugs are

....

18.

Things that make you YOU

(Complete each line with a word or phrase
beginning with the letter provided.)

G ....

R ....

A ....

N ....

D ....

M ....

A ....

19.

If we made a movie together, we'd call it

....

and it would be about

....

20.

One of my favorite outdoor activities is

....

because you

....

21.

I'm proud of you for

. . . .

22.

I hope you're proud of me for

. . . .

"extra love"

23.

Your

....

and

....

are better than anyone else's.

24.

The top three things that make you different from other grandmas are . . .

1. ....

2. ....

3. ....

25.

I CAN'T WAIT UNTIL WE

....

AGAIN.

26.

You are the only one who

....

27.

If you were an animal, you'd be a

. . . .

28.

The top three ways I'm like you are . . .

1. ....

2. ....

3. ....

29.

I want to teach you

....

30.

I'm grateful you introduced me to

....

and

....

31.

I WAS SO

....

THE TIME YOU SHOWED ME

....

32.

You help me believe it's okay to

....

33.

I would love to know how you

....

34.

I think it's awesome you

....

because

....

35.

I treasure

....

 with you, especially when

....

36.

I hope I get to

....

next time I visit your house.

37.

My favorite photo of us is

....

"extra love"

38.

Thanks to you,

....

and

....

are special books to me.

39.

The top three ways I know you love me are . . .

1. ....

2. ....

3. ....

40.

Your superpower is

....

41.

WE MADE A GREAT TEAM WHEN WE

42.

You can tell we are family because

....

43.

We both like

....

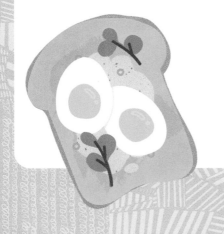

44.

We both don't like

....

45.

It means a lot to me that you support

my interest in

....

46.

I'm so glad you never

....

47.

Reasons you're the best grandma

(Complete each line with a word or phrase
beginning with the letter.)

B

E

S

T

48.

MY FAVORITE TIME WITH YOU WAS WHEN

....

49.

Your

....

is why I

....

50.

I miss your

....

when we are apart.

51.

I'm always ready to

....

with you.

52.

When I was little, I thought you

....

53.

The top three places that are special to me
because of you are . . .

1. ....

2. ....

3. ....

54.

It's easy to

....

when you

....

55.

I ENJOY WATCHING

....

WITH YOU.

56.

A perfect day together would be

....

"extra love"

57.

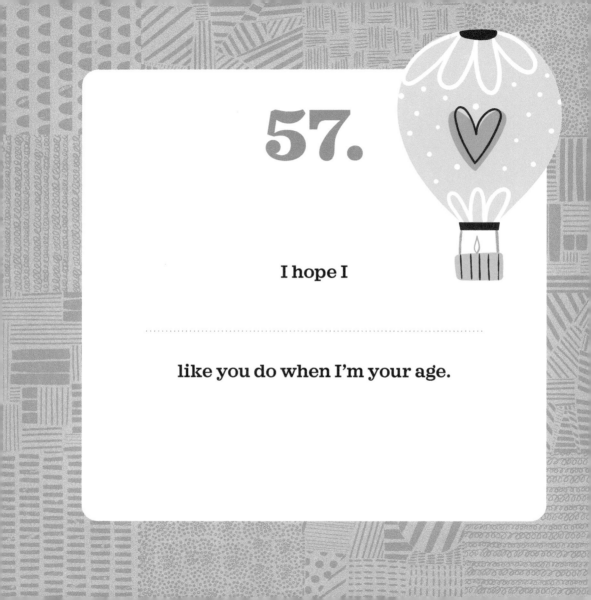

I hope I

....

like you do when I'm your age.

58.

My

....

and

....

came from you.

59.

Your advice about

....

is something I always try to follow.

60.

I'm impressed that you know a lot about

. . . .

61.

One day, I will make you

....

so you

....**.**

62.

Thank you for

....

and

....

63.

The top three things I learned from you that will help me as an adult are . . .

1. ....

2. ....

3. ....

64.

It's funny when you get happy about

. . . .

65.

I WAS THRILLED WHEN YOU

SURPRISED ME BY

....

66.

If you were a musical instrument, you'd be a

....

because

....

67.

The top three new things we should try together are . . .

1. ....

2. ....

3. ....

68.

You are fantastic at

....

because

....

69.

THE LAST TIME WE

....

TOGETHER, I FELT

....

70.

I want you to teach me

·· .

71.

I like how your eyes

....

72.

I want you to

....

when I grow up.

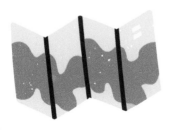

73.

I know the words

....

and

....

because of you.

74.

The scent of

....

makes me think of you.

75.

I never thanked you for

.... ,

and I want to say

....

76.

EVERY TIME I

.... ,

I REMEMBER WHEN WE

....

77.

I want to help you with

....

when I'm older.

"extra love"

78.

The top three things I know you like to do
with me are . . .

1. ....

2. ....

3. ....

79.

Every time you joke about

....,

I can't help but

....

80.

I hope someone takes a picture of us when we

....

so we always remember it.

81.

I'm grateful we respect our differences. You

love me even though I

....

and you don't.

82.

I love you even though you

....

and I don't.

83.

One thing that makes you weird in a

good way is

....

84.

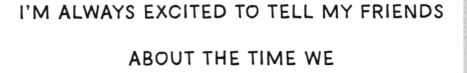

I'M ALWAYS EXCITED TO TELL MY FRIENDS

ABOUT THE TIME WE

·· .

85.

The top three songs that make me think of you are . . .

1. ....

2. ....

3. ....

86.

Our relationship is unique because

....

87.

If I could give you anything in the world,

I'd give you

....

88.

I appreciate seeing

....

and

....

because of you.

89.

I'm glad you were there the first time I

....

90.

When I hear your voice, I

....

91.

I SMILE WHEN I REMEMBER THE TIME

THAT WE LAUGHED EXTRA HARD ABOUT

....

92.

You helped me

....

and I'm grateful for that.

93.

Ways I can show you how much I love you

(Complete each line with a word or phrase
beginning with the letter.)

L ....

O ....

V ....

E ....

94.

A FUN GAME WE PLAY TOGETHER IS

....

95.

I like to call you

....

because it reminds me that

....

96.

I always wonder how you

....

97.

One thing I hope you always remember about

you and me is

....

98.

I know that when you were my age,

you loved to

....

99.

I'm impressed you hope to

one day.

100.

The top three things the world should know about you are . . .

1. ....

2. ....

3. ....

CPSIA information can be obtained
at www.ICGtesting.com
Printed in the USA
JSHW030310091121
20306JS00006B/11

9 781638 073437